THE HISPANIC INFLUENCE IN THE UNITED STATES

LATINOS
IN AMERICAN HISTORY

JUAN BAUTISTA DE ANZA

BY JOHN BANKSTON

Mitchell Lane
PUBLISHERS

P.O. Box 196
Hockessin, Delaware 19707

THE HISPANIC INFLUENCE IN THE UNITED STATES

LATINOS
IN AMERICAN HISTORY

OTHER TITLES IN THE SERIES

Visit us on the web: www.mitchelllane.com
Comments? email us: mitchelllane@mitchelllane.com

THE HISPANIC INFLUENCE IN THE UNITED STATES

LATIN?S
IN AMERICAN HISTORY

JUAN BAUTISTA
DE ANZA

BY JOHN BANKSTON

Printing 1   2   3   4   5   6   7   8   9

Library of Congress Cataloging-in-Publication Data

Bankston, John, 1974-
     Juan Bautista de Anza / by John Bankston.
                         p. cm. — (Latinos in American history)
Summary: A biography of explorer Juan Bautista de Anza, who established a land route
     between Mexico and California and became governor of New Mexico.
Includes bibliographical references and index.
     ISBN 1-58415-196-X (Library Bound)
     1. Anza, Juan Bautista de, 1735-1788—Juvenile literature. 2. California—Discovery and
     exploration—Spanish—Juvenile literature. 3. Southwest, New—Discovery and explora-
     tion—Spanish—Juvenile literature. 4. Explorers—California—Biography—Juvenile
     literature. 5. Explorers—Southwest, New—Biography—Juvenile literature. 6. Explor-
     ers—Spain—Biography—Juvenile literature. [1. Anza, Juan Bautista de, 1735-1788. 2.
     Explorers. 3. Governors. 4. California—History—To 1846. 5. Southwest, New—History—
     To 1848.] I. Title. II. Series.
     F864 .A575 2003
     979'.01'092--dc21
                                                                              2002153207

ABOUT THE AUTHOR: Born in Boston, Massachussetts, John Bankston began publishing articles in newspapers and magazines while still a teenager. Since then, he has written over two hundred articles, and contributed chapters to books such as *Crimes of Passion*, and *Death Row 2000*, which have been sold in bookstores across the world. He has written numerous biographies for young adults, including *Mandy Moore* and *Alexander Fleming and the Story of Penicillin* (Mitchell Lane). He currently lives in Portland, Oregon.

PHOTO CREDITS: Cover: National Park Service; p. 6 Corbis; p. 10 Archivo Iconografico, S.A./Corbis; p. 16 National Park Service; p. 20 Stephanie Kondrchek; p. 24 North Wind Picture Archive; p. 26 Bettmann/Corbis; p. 28 Gordon Burhop; p. 34 Jan Butchofsky-Houser/ Corbis; p. 36 Cal Peters/National Park Service

PUBLISHER'S NOTE: This story is based on the author's extensive research, which he believes to be accurate. Documentation of this research can be found on page 45. Some parts of the text might have been created by the author based on his research to illustrate what might have happened years ago, and is solely an aid to readability for young adults.

     The spelling of the names in this book follow the generally accepted usage of modern day. The spelling of Spanish names in English has evolved over time with no consistency. Many names have been anglicized and no longer use the accent marks or any Spanish grammar. Others have retained the Spanish grammar. Hence, we refer to Hernando De Soto as "De Soto," but Francisco Vásquez de Coronado as "Coronado." There are other variances as well. Some sources might spell Vásquez as Vazquez. For the most part, we have adapted the more widely recognized spellings.

CONTENTS

Although Spanish explorers endured everything from harsh weather to lack of food, few things slowed their progress more than Apache attacks. Anza's father died in one of their raids; in this illustration women and children are held prisoner — men were usually killed immediately.

A BRUTAL BATTLE

The Apaches attacked.

They rode on horses they'd bred and horses stolen from the Spanish settlers and soldiers. It was a spring day in 1740, and Juan Bautista de Anza was unprepared. The cautious captain never rode along the ridges and canyons without protection. But when he reached the open country, he felt safe.

He was wrong.

Before his soldiers could save him, Juan lay dead. The Apaches had attacked quickly, then moved on.

From their mounts or sheltered positions, the Apaches carefully aimed their bows. The arrows they launched were over two feet long, tipped with eagle or turkey feathers on one end and deadly barbed arrowheads on the other. The arrowhead lay flat against the arrow's shaft. When fired, it hit horizontally—driving between a victim's ribs, piercing the internal organs.

Apache warriors hardly ever missed. They could hit a moving target up to 150 yards away. And when their arrows found their mark, the victim had less than thirty minutes before the glue between the shaft and arrowhead dissolved. That left the arrowhead firmly embedded inside the victim's body.

Death was almost certain.

For well over 200 years following Christopher Columbus' discovery of the New World, Spanish conquistadors—conquerors—had taken over the land of the natives they encountered with little or no difficulty. However, few tribes were as fierce as the Apaches. This group of Native Americans was as responsible as the harsh desert for Spain's lack of interest in settling much of the area north of Mexico.

Long before the Spanish arrival in the New World—which was marked by the explorations of men like Columbus, Hernando de Soto and Juan Rodríguez Cabrillo—the Apaches had moved southward through North America. Their ancestors had migrated to North America during the most recent Ice Age. That was a period thousands of years ago when temperatures across the globe plummeted. Tundra and snow covered much of the planet. During the Ice Age a strip of land known as the Beringia connected what is now Siberia and Alaska. The Beringia offered a land bridge for primitive people to travel from Asia to North America. Eventually they spread throughout much of the continent. When European explorers reached the New World, Native Americans had lived there for thousands of years.

By the 1500s, Apaches began trekking from what is now Western Canada into modern-day Texas, New Mexico, and Arizona. In the 1600s, Apache aggression increased as they battled neighboring tribes, enslaving their members and increasing their own numbers.

Their aggression had a purpose. The Apaches needed horses and supplies and got them by raiding the Spanish.

In the border areas of New Spain (Mexico) the Spanish began pushing north. They had already marched through much of Mexico and what is today South America. The Spanish conquered such warrior tribes as the Aztecs, and enslaved the

Mayans. They turned vast stretches of New Spain into farmland and mining operations. They built missions and small towns surrounded by ranches and other dwellings.

But their string of relatively easy conquests was threatened by the Apaches. The Apaches made explorations and settlements beyond the border of New Spain much more difficult.

They were fearsome warriors. Dressed in broad skin loincloths, bare-chested in the summer and wearing long buckskin shirts in the winter, they seemed immune from the harsh effects of heat or cold. They were able to go for days without food and could survive the desert sun with little water. Late at night, beneath the light of a full moon, small bands attacked quickly. They raided the Spanish outposts and then disappeared. Their fighting tactics were part of why the Spanish scarcely explored the territories they'd discovered.

Indeed, the Apaches would continue to battle settlers and soldiers—Spanish, Mexican and American—until well into the 1800s.

Anza hoped to help the Spanish develop their territory. He dreamed of exploring and developing a land route connecting Mexico to the Pacific coast area first explored by Juan Rodriguez Cabrillo nearly 200 years earlier. Anza pleaded with the rulers in Spain and the governors in Mexico. He tried desperately to convince them of the value of his plan. For a long time they resisted.

The dream of his lifetime ended with the Apache attack. After years of fighting the tribes, Anza's luck ran out.

But his dream did not die with him. Anza left behind a son, a toddler who would grow up to fulfill his father's ambition.

The boy's name, like his father's, was Juan Bautista de Anza. His work to develop a land route between Mexico and California made him a significant influence in California history.■

Looking for a trade route, Christopher Columbus instead found a path to the New World. His discovery led to the arrival of explorers, most of them hungry for adventure and riches.

THE FATHER'S DREAM

The discovery of America had been accidental. Explorers like Christopher Columbus were seeking trade routes, not land. But every decade brought further exploration into the "New World," what would soon become known as North and South America. To Europeans, the area inside the future continental United States seemed filled with promise. The land offered unexplored, unconquered territory, and—above all—wealth for anyone brave enough to risk the dangerous voyage across the Atlantic.

By the 1700s, after the great age of the early explorations, the territories of the New World provided unrivaled opportunities. The younger Juan Bautista de Anza was a member of a new generation of Spanish settlers, the children of merchants and soldiers, farmers and ranchers who came of age in what would become the United States and Mexico. The area wasn't the New World to this new generation.

It was home.

Both Juan's father, Juan Bautista de Anza, Sr. and his grandfather Antonio Bezerra Nieto had been presidio captains. Soon Juan would join this noble military tradition.

Like many Spanish in the 18th century, his father moved to the New World dreaming of wealth and adventure. He found both. And like many who arrived in the Americas during this period, he also found an early death.

Although the family had a drug store in Spain, when Anza's father arrived in the New World in 1712 at the age of nineteen he had very little money. He later built a great reputation in the military as captain of the presidio in Janos, Chihuahua and in Fronteras near the modern border between Mexico and Arizona. He rode with the cavalry, engaging native tribes in battle. By the time he died, he'd developed mines, built ranches and started stores to serve the needs of local settlers. Little Juan lost a father but gained a great inheritance.

Juan was born sometime in the middle of 1736 at either the Fronteras Presidio or in Cuquiárachi in the province of Sonora. On July 7th he was baptized in Cuquiárachi. Less than four years later, his father was dead.

The tiny mission church sat atop a hill overlooking a creek. As Father Rojas performed the baptism Juan's mother and father, Juan and María Rosa viewed the ceremony beside their five other children. The service was described in Volume One of *Anza's California Expeditions,*

"This new baby would never know any of his grandparents or family in the old country but, like the ceremony of baptism itself, this was a new beginning. The Día de San Juan, or feast day of John the Baptist, had fallen on Sunday that year. So, like his Father before him, the weeklong ceremonies commemorating this beloved Saint had ended on the Saturday previous to the new baby's baptism. It was appropriate that he should be given the same name as his Father. It was appropriate that he should be given the name of St. John the Baptist. Especially in this desert country, where rain was so scarce, it was appropriate that he be given a name associated with water and the beginning of the rainy season. It was a joyous day."

Juan grew up on the Guevavi Mission, on the Divisadero Ranch which his mother, María Rosa Bezerra Nieto, bought after her husband's death. Nothing provided better training for a military and exploring career than an adolescent life among horses and cattle. He learned to rope; he learned to ride.

As a youngster, Juan must have heard countless stories of his father's adventures from his mother, from the vaqueros (cowboys) on the ranch and from the soldiers who'd served under the senior Juan Anza's command. He heard stories about his father's experiences in the cavalry and the battles he fought against Apaches in the borderlands around what is now Arizona.

He also heard about the dream his father carried to the grave. The dream to explore and develop a land route from Mexico to California.

In the mid-1700s, the Spanish began to re-focus their attentions on the western coastline of North America. Two hundred years before, Juan Rodríguez Cabrillo had made a fateful and ultimately fatal trip along that coast. Before he died, he discovered the magnificent bay of San Diego and sailed north toward Oregon.

Yet despite the work of Cabrillo and the conquistadors who followed, much of the western United States was largely unexplored territory. Along the eastern seaboard, British colonists developed cities like Boston, Baltimore, Philadelphia and New York which grew into thriving young metropolises. Between the rugged Appalachian mountains and the massive Mississippi River, the French had staked their claims, building towns and developing commerce from Canada to Louisiana.

The Spanish had to make do with deserts.

Though Mexico City was the largest city in North America, the Spanish believed that the land from the Pacific Ocean to the

Mississippi was too arid and difficult to farm. Native tribes like the Apaches were often violent. So developing the land they'd discovered decades—even centuries before—was not a priority to Spain's rulers.

Until the Russians arrived.

Between 1725 and 1740, a Danish sea captain named Vitus Bering began a series of explorations for the Russians. Like Christopher Columbus, like many of the early explorers, Bering's goals and his accomplishments became two very different things.

For years there were rumors of a connecting body of water—a strait—between the Atlantic and the Pacific Oceans. The Spanish, unaware of the true size of the American continent, were convinced the strait ran somewhere along the northern part of New Spain, or Mexico. The Russians were sure the body of water between Russia and what would one day be called Alaska contained this strait.

In truth this route was a myth. But many explorers and the hapless sailors who went with them died trying to find it.

Bering sailed up Russia's eastern coast right into the Arctic Ocean, and discovered what would later be called the Bering Strait. This area between Russia's Siberia and the future state of Alaska was separated by only a few miles of icy water. Bering's other discoveries would provide Mother Russia with a direct path to the New World and the riches the land promised.

After Bering's death, other Russians followed his maps and his journeys. Over the next few decades, they established settlements on the Aleutian islands and the mainland that extended down the Alaskan coast for nearly a thousand miles. Russian ships even began cruising along the Washington and Oregon coastline. Soon they would venture even further south, to California.

So the Spanish rulers were nervous.

"The High Government of Spain being informed of the repeated attempts of a foreign nation upon the northern coasts of

California with aims by no means favorable to the Monarchy and its interests [the governor of California and his men] should take effective measures to guard that part of his dominions from invasion and insult," the Spanish government would say early in 1768. They directed the leaders in Mexico to begin building settlements in what became known as Alta, or upper, California.

They already had some scattered settlements in Baja, or lower, California. But there was nothing further north.

The main reason was that there were enormous difficulties in trying to build settlements with supplies brought from the sea. Sea voyages typically lasted for months, and everyone aboard faced the dangers of scurvy. That was a disease caused by a lack of vitamin C (a vitamin found in citrus fruits like lemons and oranges), which caused bleeding under the skin and extreme weakness, even death. Since 18th century sailors didn't have the ability to store food like we do today, scurvy was a persistent worry.

Clearly, establishing and supplying settlements from the ocean was not the best choice. Though a land route seemed to provide the best solution, Juan's father had met resistance when he proposed such a route. His motivations in the 1730s were based as much in exploration as practicality.

The Russian threat several decades later provided the Spanish government with its own motivation. Supplying the settlers by land would make sense. After all, settlements and missions could be developed along the way. With work an unbroken line of farms and ranches could supply the west coast settlements. That would keep the Russians where they belonged—far away from California.

In the meantime, Juan was a teenager. He may have dreamed of living the rest of his life on his ranch.

But his reality lay in the military tradition of his family. His future involved wearing an officer's uniform and fighting the same Apaches who had killed his father.■

Although this painting of Anza is probably not an accurate depiction of him, it shows the presidio commander sitting proudly atop a horse, while in the background the rest of his party waits.

APACHE FIGHTER

It wasn't surprising that Juan became a soldier. In addition to his father's legacy, his grandfather on his mother's side had been a presidio captain for 30 years. So the youngster began his military career at the age of 16 as a volunteer, instead of one of the presidial companies supported by the crown that paid wages. Like all soldiers on the frontier, he had to supply his own horse and weapons. In the 18th century joining the army at such a young age was quite common.

Three years later he had his first posting. It was at Fronteras, the same presidio his father had commanded and where he had been born. This posting was still a family affair, for his immediate commander was his sister's husband, Gabriel de Vildosola. Captain Vildosola was a presidial captain.

The cavalry was an organized force of soldiers on horseback. Horses had been an essential element to Spanish success, more valuable even than cannons or muskets. Mounted on their horses, the first conquistadors were fearsome opponents. Native tribesmen who had never seen horses sometimes thought they were being attacked by a single giant beast, instead of a separate animal and its rider. In Cuba and in Mexico, the Spanish sometimes even claimed victory without having to fight. The natives surrendered before the battle even began.

But by the time Juan joined the cavalry, the horse was no longer a mythical beast to many of the tribes. By then, the theft of horses by neighboring tribes had become a major problem for many presidios. In fact, horse thieves would even slow down Juan Anza's future ambitions.

Juan's skills as a soldier and fighter quickly became legendary. Under his brother-in-law's command, Juan took part in a number of campaigns against the Apaches. He might have wondered if the men he was attacking were the same ones who killed his father.

Juan was later described by those who rode alongside him as an uncanny warrior—he seemed able to know what the Apaches would do before they did it. He seemed to know what they were thinking, what their plans were. During his time in the cavalry he became schooled in Apache tactics. He learned to track as well as a native, to match their own physical endurance and most of all, to fight like they did.

In one campaign he took part in a battle which left 40 Apaches dead and over 200 captured. In another, he led a detachment of soldiers and native allies who stormed an Apache position in the shadows of the Chiracahua Mountains. Not only were a number of Apaches killed, but Juan also took back cattle which had been stolen from the presidio.

Single-handedly, Juan took the Apache chief prisoner.

South of Fronteras, Juan took part in a number of campaigns against the Seris, another fierce tribe. These battles cemented his reputation as a fearsome Indian-fighter. He was promoted to lieutenant in 1756.

So as he entered his twenties, Juan Anza was battle-scarred and well-trained in the art of frontier warfare. He was also about to come across a major opportunity.

Deep into the borderlands, where the Santa Cruz River cuts into what is today Southern Arizona, lies the town of Tubac. In 1752 a presidio was established there after a brief rebellion of the Pima tribe. It became the first permanent European settlement in present-day Arizona. Outside the presidio every step was a dangerous one. The presidio rested in a valley and quickly became the bulls-eye for native aggression with the war-like Apache tribes to the east.

Its first captain, Juan de Belderrain, was hit by a poisoned arrow while fighting the Seris on Tiburón Island in the Gulf of California. He survived long enough to return to the presidio and relinquish command.

On December 7, 1759, Juan Anza was made captain of the presidio at Tubac and put in charge of the entire compound. Juan was twenty-four years old, and very soon he would have a chance to prove himself.■

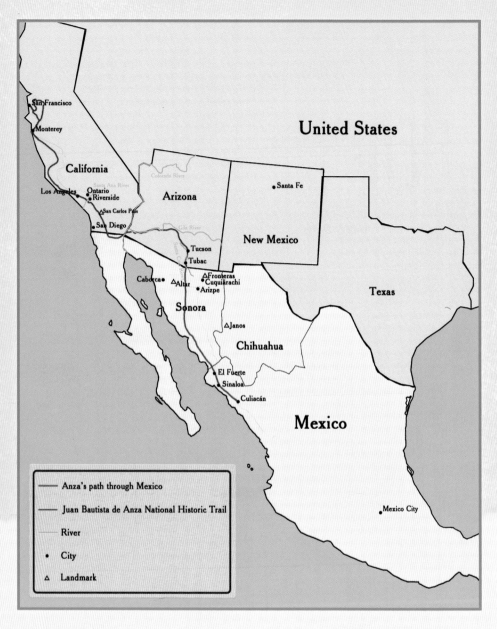

Trying to fulfill his father's dreams, Anza traveled further than the
senior Anza could imagine. This map illustrates his route through
Mexico and the Juan Bautista de Anza National Historic Trail, the
path he established from Mexico to the California coast.

PEACE!

By the time Juan Anza took command of the Tubac presidio, he faced a rebellion. Ciprian of the Pima tribe refused to give in to Spanish rule. In the spring of 1760, he and several of his followers attacked. Tribesmen entered the presidio, killing soldiers and stealing horses. Before the Spanish could counter, the Indians retreated, returning to the safety of their homes.

But although Juan was new to his command, he wasn't about to go home in disgrace. He organized the cavalry, and gave them orders to attack the Pimas. And Juan Anza didn't just send his men into combat.

He joined them.

The battle was brutal. Warfare in the 18th century could be fought from a distance—with guns and cannons, or bow and arrows. But it could also be fought close-up with swords and knives, hand-to-hand, face-to-face.

Juan and his men killed eight Pima warriors. Then he faced Chief Ciprian. In violent hand-to-hand combat, the young presidio captain killed Ciprian. The event was a turning point in the relationship between the Spanish and the tribes of the borderlands.

Juan didn't spend all of his time fighting. He also fell in love with a young woman he had known since childhood. Her name was Doña Ana María Pérez Serrano, and after a period of courtship, the couple married on June 24, 1761.

Over the next decade Juan worked hard to bring peace to an area which had only known war. He was willing to fight for his objectives, but he insisted that his men treat the natives fairly. He refused to engage in the types of brutal conquests which had soured the relations between Spanish and native tribes for decades. He won campaigns against the Seris, the Suaquis and the Apaches.

Although Juan was praised for his courage in battle, he wasn't the perfect commander. His frequent trips away from the fort left many of the soldiers there feeling like children with an absent father. Worse, the men he appointed to take charge in his absence were often poorly suited for the job. Ensign Huandurraga and Sergeant Marques were especially hated for the cruel way they disciplined the lower ranking soldiers. It was a time when flogging and branding were common means of punishment, but these two even used swords!

Still, when Juan was in Tubac, he ran a disciplined and orderly presidio. He was singled out for praise by Field Marshal Marqués de Rubí who noted that Juan didn't try to make money by selling goods to his soldiers. This was different from many other presidio commanders, who charged high prices to their troops. The unfortunate men didn't have anywhere else to shop, so they had to pay whatever their commanders charged. Despite his lack of wealth, Juan refused to take advantage of his soldiers. But many men richer than he were made extra money by over-charging the soldiers under their command. "This act," Rubí noted in his official report, "which shows a generosity rare in these lands, makes this officer worthy of experiencing the effects of the royal gratitude."

Yet even as he won victories in battle, a familiar dream returned to Juan. It began as a rumor.

Juan started to hear stories of white men traveling up and down the Pacific coast, hundreds of miles away. He didn't hear these stories from other Spanish men. He heard them from the native Pimas. They in turn had heard them from tribes who lived "on the other side of the Colorado [River], at some distance," Juan would later recall. "White men were passing, a thing which they had never seen before—this tribe repeated the story to the very reverend father Fray Francisco Garcés."

The rumors were based on solid fact. In the late spring of 1769, a Spanish expedition under the command of Gaspar de Portolá had founded a tiny settlement at San Diego in Alta, or upper, California. The following year, the Portolá expedition reached Monterey, 400 miles to the north, and established another settlement.

The news excited Juan. The land between Tubac and the Pacific Ocean was believed to be a vast expanse of impassable desert and mountains. If stories about the explorers were able to travel backwards to his presidio, why couldn't explorers make the journey forward—from the borderlands right into California?

Any doubts that he may have had were removed by Father Garcés. An acquaintance of Anza's, he was a missionary who had established good relations with many of the Indian tribes even though he was still a young man in his mid-thirties. He wanted to check out these stories personally. So without any companions, he followed the Gila River to where it joined the Colorado River. There he made friends with Palma, the chief of the Yuma Indians.

Garcés went downstream along the Colorado River almost to the Sea of Cortez, then struck out northwest across the desert. Near the present-day Mexican border, he began following a series of valleys between mountain ranges. Eventually he could see what he was sure was a gap in the mountains far off in the distance. That gap, he believed, would provide a way of reaching the Spanish mission at San Gabriel, which is located to the east of modern-day Los Angeles. From there, it would be relatively easy to continue on to Monterey, what was then the northernmost

Gaspar de Portolá's explorations led to the first Spanish towns in what would become California – future cities like San Diego and Monterey. This painting may not be an accurate portrayal of Gaspar de Portolá.

Spanish settlement in Alta California. When Garcés returned, he described his travels to Juan.

Juan realized that the time to make his father's dreams come true had arrived. Viceroy Antonio Bucareli came to Mexico to question the participants of the journey. On May 2, 1772, Juan wrote one of the most important letters of his life. It began: "The fervent desire which at all times moves me to serve his Majesty and advance his conquests, impels me to beg of your Excellency, in case you learn that it is to be granted to anyone, permission to make the necessary efforts to see we can open communication between the port of Monte Rey (Monterey) and the province of Sonora."

The letter was taken by horseback to Mexico City. An engineer named Miguel Costanso, who had been a member of the Portolá expedition, confirmed Juan's belief. He estimated that the distance between Tubac and San Diego was less than 600 miles—considerably shorter than what had been believed for many years.

He said that the mountains would present a problem, but added that "some openings were seen, and since the Indians cross them easily, our people will be able to do likewise."

Juan had another ally: Father Junípero Serra. He had also accompanied Portolá and was the leader of the Franciscan missions that had been established in California. He happened to be in Mexico City, speaking with Bucareli about his concerns, when Anza's letter arrived.

Father Serra brought first-hand knowledge of how dangerous and slender Spain's hold on Alta California was. At that time there were just two presidios—Monterey and San Diego—and three additional missions—San Gabriel, San Luis Obispo and San Antonio. All told, they contained only about 70 Spanish settlers.

One of the main reasons for the sparse numbers was that it was very difficult to supply the new settlements. Supplies had to be carried hundreds of miles overland in Mexico, then loaded onto tiny sailing ships. These ships then faced a voyage of—

Seasoned explorer and respected priest, Junípero Serra's religious mission served Spain's dreams of western settlements. He rode alongside several military commanders, including Anza.

under ideal circumstances—two or three months. It could take longer. Or forever. Portolá's expedition several years earlier had been placed in grave danger when one supply ship disappeared without a trace. And things hadn't gotten much better. The arrival of the supply ships once or twice a year always led to celebration and happiness.

A land route, Anza suggested, would make it easier to bring more supplies. It would also be more dependable.

Despite this show of support for Juan's plan, Viceroy Bucareli took a long time to make his decision. And all Juan could do was wait. ■

Camino del Diablo — the Devil's Highway — stretched one hundred miles through the mountains. A parched strip of land in barren desert, the "highway" was one of the most dangerous portions of a very dangerous journey.

ANZA SETS OUT

Sebastián Tarabal emerged from the desert near the presidio of Altar in Sonora, located to the southwest of Tubac. He was exhausted, near death, covered in the dust of his journey. To the soldiers and settlers in Altar he probably looked like a ghost.

He wasn't.

It was late in 1773 when he arrived from the barren reaches of the borderlands. His arrival would confirm Juan Anza's theory. The desert was smaller than many Spanish explorers had believed.

Tarabal had abandoned the newly created mission at San Gabriel a few months before. A member of one of the Native American tribes of Baja (lower) California, he'd made the journey north to help found the mission. But Tarabal hated the structure of mission life, and soon fled with his wife and a friend.

Their journey was arduous. The trio was terrified of the unfamiliar tribes which called the region home, but in the end it was the desert heat and not an attack which cost Tarabal's wife and his friend their lives.

Tarabal arrived alone, just as Anza was planning his journey. He'd finally received approval from the viceroy in Mexico. Although Juan would have to pay for most of the trip's expenses, he didn't care. He financed the trip with borrowed money.

He was thirty-seven years old and about to embark on the journey he'd been preparing for his whole life.

Unfortunately problems developed even before the trip began. Although skirmishes with the surrounding native tribes had been greatly reduced by Juan's command, the Apaches still caused difficulty. The Spanish garrison was raided frequently for supplies and horses. Besides occasionally killing the odd Spanish soldier, the Apaches were brilliant thieves.

Coincidentally, one of their most daring raids occurred in early January of 1774, just one week before Juan and his men were about to make their trip. Under night's cover, Apache warriors sneaked into the Tubac Presidio's herd of spare horses and stole many of the horses intended for the trip.

It was a devastating blow. But Juan Anza was not about to be stopped so easily. He'd planned on going north. Now he'd just start the trip by going south to resupply.

So the journey began on January 9, 1774. Accompanying Juan were 21 soldiers, five mule packers, an interpreter and a carpenter. He also brought along two personal servants. He may have been leaving on the trip of a lifetime, but he wasn't about to suffer needlessly.

Along with the soldiers, he brought two Franciscan priests—Father Juan Díaz and Father Garcés, missionaries whose goals were based on Catholicism, not explorations. Men like Fathers Díaz and Garcés helped Native Americans learn new farming methods, taught them to read, write and when necessary protected them from Spanish soldiers.

Also with the group was Sebastián Tarabal, who would now act as a guide.

The Apache theft extracted its price in time and distance. The men had to travel south to Caborca, 125 miles out of their way, to seek replacement mounts.

What they found there did not meet their expectations. The horses were underfed, the cattle weak. Any animal they brought would probably die on the way. So most of the 140 horses, 65 head of cattle and three dozen mules came from the Tubac presidio, as Anza only took a few animals from Caborca. For a journey which would last well over one thousand miles, their supplies were very meager.

After spending time in Caborca, the group headed northwest toward the Colorado River. They crossed through an area controlled by the Papago tribe. As Juan noted in his journal on January 23, "Papagos are not the people most hostile towards us, as we have experienced on the few occasions when they have revolted—they have paid dearly before the fury of arms."

Clearly Juan believed his policies were working—and since none of the tribes they encountered showed any aggression, he had no reason to believe otherwise.

By then the men had seen unbelievable sights, including giant cacti called saguaros, which were fifty feet high. Their fruit was used by the natives to make a thick syrup they turned into a strong alcoholic drink.

Then they entered the hardest part of the journey, about 100 miles through rugged mountains, a path that was later called Camino del Diablo, or the Devil's Highway. The men survived by drinking from natural water tanks—large, hollow indentations in the rock formations which collected rainwater.

As peaceful as the Papagos had been, the natives around the area where Yuma, Arizona is today were even more receptive to the Spanish. Father Garcés had done his work well. Juan's party arrived on February 7th. They'd traveled nearly 400 miles. Greeting Yuma's Chief Palma, Anza told the tribesmen that "in the name of the king who was lord of everybody, I was confirming him [Palma] in his office, in order that he might rule legally and with greater authority, and be recognized even by the Spaniards."

Juan gave Chief Palma a red ribbon with a coin of the king to confirm the honor. He also told Palma that Spanish King Carlos III wished his people to live peaceably with the neighboring tribes.

The chief and the Yumas helped Juan and his men make the dangerous crossing over the area where the Gila and Colorado Rivers met. After fighting current and confusion— and more than a few scared men who didn't know how to swim—the Anza party ran into major difficulties.

At this point in their journey, San Diego was just over one hundred miles away—in a straight line to the west. Their first objective, the mission at San Gabriel, was less than 100 miles from San Diego—in a straight line north.

But they couldn't head directly west because of huge sand dunes that were virtually impassable. So they headed south, intending to skirt the dunes. But soon they realized that they were lost. Tarabal's memory wasn't accurate, and an Indian guide ran away.

The exhausted men didn't seem to be getting any closer to Signal Mountain as they tried to find a path through the dunes for days on end. They quickly gave it a nickname: Cerro del Imposible, the Impossible Hill. Finally Anza made a decision. He sent part of the expedition back to Yuma with many of their supplies.

The slimmed-down expedition, now about 20 men, headed even further south. They soon escaped the dunes and were able to head back north. Signal Mountain finally lived up to its name. The men found a gap in the mountains just to its left and crossed the modern-day border between California and Mexico.

Then they arrived at an area where the San Felipe and Carrizo Creeks met, forming a marshy area. He named the marsh San Sebastián after Saint Sebastián.

On March 12, 1774, the group reached Borrego Spring. They headed north along Coyote Creek, crossing through Cahuilla tribes land and cutting through a pass which ran between the Santa Rosa and San Jacinto Mountains.

By then the men realized they were close to Monterey.

At San Carlos pass, 4000 thousand feet above sea level, Juan recorded his thoughts, "From it are seen the most beautiful green and flower-strewn prairies and snow covered mountains with pines, oaks and other trees which grow in cold countries."

They descended and passed through the sites of modern California cities such as Riverside and Ontario. He reached the San Gabriel Mission on March 22. His men were unexpected.

"We found here four friars, its missionaries, from the College of San Fernando de Mexico, who welcomed us with unrestrained jubilation and joy," Juan later wrote.

Juan again reduced the number of men with him, making the trip to Monterey with only four soldiers and two men from San Gabriel who guided the group. The trip to Monterey was by now a familiar one, having previously been made by Portolá.

Juan Bautista de Anza had done it! He'd made his father's dream come true and in the process, his own ambitions as well. Except he wasn't done. Sure, he'd proven the trip could be made with a group of soldiers.

The big challenge was to do it with women and children. Could he make the trip with families willing to re-settle in Monterey? There was only one way to find out. And it wasn't going to be easy.■

From presidio commander to governor of New Mexico, Anza was going to command the Buenaventura Presidio when he died unexpectedly. He was buried here, at Nuestra Señora de Loreto.

CHAPTER
6

FINAL JOURNEYS

In May of 1774, Juan returned to his presidio at Tubac. He received a hero's welcome. He'd found a land route to Monterey. That was something that many people had dreamed of, including his own father. For his bravery and service to the crown, he was promoted in rank to lieutenant colonel.

Already he was planning his next expedition.

The countries which had claimed portions of North America followed a kind of "finders keepers" type of rule. Whoever "found" a piece of land could "keep" it for his home country. This was called a claim and along the western coast Spanish claims stretched all the way to Oregon.

The problem was the Russians. Following Captain Bering's discovery, Russian settlements had begun extending southward. It was only a matter of time before they reached the edge of Spanish territory. Although the land had been claimed by Spain for over two centuries, most of the area was scarcely populated. Even as far south as San Diego, the population numbered in the dozens. In order to keep the Russians out, the Spanish realized

Just as today, the poor of the 18th century dreamed of a better life. Many were willing to risk everything for opportunities. Here Anza and his recruits set off from Tubac. Though this painting shows the men in red uniforms with blue trim, the actual uniforms were blue with red trim.

they needed real settlements: missions and presidios, ranches and farms.

That would take people.

However, convincing people to make the dangerous journey to the west coast and live in an area where supplies were scarce wasn't easy. There weren't many people willing to abandon their homes for possible starvation.

Juan had a solution.

Following his hero's welcome in Tubac, he was ordered to take charge of the Presidio of Terrenate. In November, he traveled south towards Mexico City. He stopped at every presidio along the way, getting a fresh horse, and telling tales of his journey. Even as he rode, Juan was planning.

In a letter to the viceroy, Anza described the kinds of people he needed: "submerged in the direst poverty and misery, they would most willingly and gladly embrace the advantages which your Excellency may deign to offer them."

On his trip toward Mexico City, Juan found exactly the type of people he needed. They lived in the towns of Culiacán, Sinaloa and El Fuerte. They were poor and they were desperate. They would also have to be outfitted in every way, "from shoes to hair ribbons," as Juan told the viceroy.

At a council in Mexico City, it was decided to fund the mission. People would be sent to build a settlement near San Francisco Bay. They would be given supplies, clothing, and silver.

After getting the viceroy's permission, Juan began his recruitment. He may have told the residents of Culiacán about the opportunities that lay further to the west, described the beauty of the coast to the villagers of Sinaloa or the great possible riches to the people in El Fuerte. Regardless of exactly what he told them, Juan had to be part conquering hero and part salesman.

He proved to be very convincing.

In the end nearly 200 people—half of them women and children—joined up. It wasn't an easy decision. They knew that even if the expedition was successful and they didn't die along the way, they would never return.

Juan also found more people willing to accompany the expedition as animal herders, servants, and interpreters. He also recruited some soldiers who were willing to accompany the expedition, help them found the new settlement and stay there to guard it. Altogether, about 300 people went along on the expediton. Slowly they all made their way north, halting for the summer of 1775 in the town of Horcasitas. There the "raw recruits" trained, learning how to survive in the desert and how to defend themselves against Apache attacks.

Then they continued on to Tubac, where the long-awaited journey began on October 23. Unfortunately, an Apache raid a few weeks earlier had taken nearly 500 horses which had been set aside for the expedition. That meant that Juan set out with no fresh mounts.

Accompanying Juan was Juan Pablo Grijalva, a sergeant and Don Jose Moraga, who would be a lieutenant at the Fronteras

Presidio. He would be Juan's second in command. The three all shared a tragic history—both had lost fathers to Apache attacks.

The expedition also included Father Pedro Font. Although he would suffer illness and discouragement throughout the expedition—in addition to numerous disagreements with Juan—the journal he kept provided an excellent record of the trip.

"I exhorted everybody to show perseverance and patience in the trials of so long a journey saying they ought to consider themselves happy and fortunate that God had chosen them for such an enterprise," Father Font recalled telling the group in his final mass before they left Mexico.

The trip was made without wagons or carts. All the supplies were loaded onto pack mules in the morning, and taken off every night. The supplies required for nearly 300 people and 1000 head of livestock were enormous.

The women were issued fabric for dresses, and cotton petticoats for themselves and the girls, everyone had hats and ribbons, warm winter clothes and sturdy shoes. The men had rifles and swords. They wore thick leather jackets to protect against arrows.

There were more than six tons of food. Heavy kettles and iron for making horseshoes added still more weight. Every night, wherever they rested, the group created their own small, temporary city.

And every day they struggled to avoid the Apaches.

They also avoided the Camino del Diablo by taking a slightly longer route. At first they headed north along the Santa Cruz River, reaching the area of present-day Tucson by October 26th. Five days later they arrived at the junction with the Gila River. Then they moved slowly down the Gila, arriving at its junction with the Colorado River at the end of November. They greeted Chief Palma and the rest of the friendly Yumas. The Indians helped them to carefully cross the icy cold Colorado.

After crossing the river, they formed smaller groups. That way they wouldn't exhaust the water in the springs they encountered, which took a long time to fill back up.

Still, the unexpected hovered over the group like a storm cloud. And in December, the cloud burst, covering the desert with snow. The sudden drop in temperature cost them many of their cattle, but no human lives.

They continued on in spite of the cold. There were several arguments between Juan and Father Font. The priest disapproved of Juan's habit of allowing his men to relax and drink liquor when they made camp for the night. Sometimes the two men would go for days without speaking.

On Christmas Eve, Father Font and Juan got into another argument about liquor.

"I wish to say that it does not seem to me right that we should celebrate the birth of the Infant Jesus with drunkenness," Font said.

Though Juan gave orders that the men weren't to get drunk, there was soon even more cause for celebration.

The wife of one of the soldiers gave birth to a baby boy that night. The infant, Salvador Ygnacio Linares, was the first among the Anza expedition to be born in what is now California.

The expedition spent Christmas day quietly, giving the exhausted mother some time to recover. Some of the men who may have celebrated a little too much must have welcomed the extra day as well.

The following day they reached San Carlos Pass. Five days later, they crossed the Santa Ana River, no easy task since it was at flood stage. They arrived in San Gabriel safe and sound on January 4th.

Though the hardest part of the trip was over, they remained at San Gabriel for more than a month. The Indians at the Mission San Diego had revolted, killing a priest and two soldiers. Anza led some of his soldiers south to control the rebellion. In addition, the weary travelers wanted time to rest.

So it wasn't until February 17th that they embarked on the final northward leg of their expedition. The group followed the

El Camino Real, a trail which parts of still exist today as a major California highway.

On March 10th the settlers and soldiers, livestock and priests reached Monterey. They had covered 1,600 miles from their starting point with the loss of just four lives—a woman who died in childbirth just after leaving Tubac and three men who died during an outbreak of disease at Horcasitas. This was an incredible feat for such a dangerous journey. Even more remarkable, eight babies had been born during the trip. The expedition had arrived with more people than when it departed!

On March 11th, Fray Font celebrated mass, and concluded by proclaiming, "I in the name of God and of the King our lord, give thanks to our commander, Juan Bautista de Anza for the patience, prudence and good conduct which as chief he has shown in commanding this expedition and I promise him that God will reward him for his labors."

Whether or not God rewarded Juan Anza, the leaders in Mexico and Spain certainly would. Juan spent a month with some of his soldiers, exploring the territories surrounding San Francisco Bay. He chose a site for the San Francisco Presidio and for Mission Dolores. Then Juan left Monterey.

It was a sad parting.

"When I mounted my horse in the plaza," he wrote, "the people...came to me sobbing with tears. They showered me with embraces, best wishes and praises which I do not merit."

After his departure, the settlers organized and on June 17th began settling in the area which would grow into the present-day city of San Francisco.

At home, Juan's reward from his superiors was almost immediate. He was made commander of all the troops in Sonora in 1776. The next year he was made governor of New Mexico, a position he would hold for a decade. During that time his exploits continued.

In 1778 he commanded an army of 800 men that swept across the Arkansas River to battle with the Comanche tribe. During the conflict their chief Cuerno Verde was killed, but the action led to a peace treaty—which lasted longer than any other between the Comanches and settlers.

Besides fighting, Juan embarked on humanitarian efforts, saving members of the Hopi tribe who were dying from a drought.

He also continued explorations, most notably finding a route between Arizpe, Sonora and Santa Fe, New Mexico. After being released as governor of New Mexico at his own request in 1787, he was appointed to command the Buenaventura Presidio. Before returning, however, he was appointed to command troops in Sonora and never made it to the presidio.

Sadly, Juan Anza didn't have much time to enjoy his accomplishments. After conducting a review of troops in Tucson, he returned to the home he kept in Arizpe. He died there unexpectedly on December 19, 1788. He was buried in the side chapel Nuestra Señora de Loreto of the cathedral Nuestra Señora de la Asunción of Arizpe.

In some ways, Anza's explorations are similar to what Lewis and Clark did nearly 30 years later. Both expeditions covered great distances across unknown wilderness. He also proved that not just soldiers, but entire families could endure the difficult journey across deserts and through lands belonging to native tribesmen. Before his success, this trek had been thought impossible.

But Spain would not take full advantage of his achievements. In 1781, the once-friendly Yuma Indians, provoked by Spanish intrusion of what they considered to be their land, massacred more than 50 Spaniards, including Fathers Garcés and Díaz. Without the support and cooperation of the Yumas, crossing the Colorado River was no longer possible. The trail quickly fell into disuse.

More than two centuries later, in 1990, the U.S. Congress recognized his accomplishment by creating the Juan Bautista de Anza National Historic Trail. It runs from Tubac to San Francisco. Today, travelers in their cars can cover distances in a matter of hours that Anza and his colonists took weeks to traverse.

According to the National Park Service website, "The soldiers and families that Anza escorted brought with them their language, traditions, and diverse New World Hispanic culture. Almost all the expedition members were born on this continent and had mixed European, African or Indian parentage. These influences changed the lives of the indigenous peoples and shaped the development of Arizona and California."■

CHRONOLOGY

1736   born in July in Fronteras in the Mexican province of Sonora to presidial captain Juan Bautista de Anza and Maria Rosa Bezerra Nieto

1737   father requests permission to seek land route to Alta (upper) California

1740   father is killed in Apache attack

1752   joins Spanish militia

1755   attains rank of cavalry lieutenant

1760   becomes Captain of Tubac Presidio in Sonora

1761   marries Ana María Pérez Serrano

1772   makes formal request to Viceroy Antonio Bucareli to discover land route to Alta California

1774   expedition leaves Tubac in January and travels to Monterey presidio; returns in May; promoted to lieutenant colonel because of his successful exploration

1775   leaves Tubac on October 23 with colonizing expedition

1776   expedition reaches Monterey; Anza returns to Mexico; given command of all troops in Sonora, Mexico

1777   appointed governor of New Mexico

1778   leads troops across Colorado and New Mexico, following the Colorado River to fight with Comanche Indians

1779   leads expedition to discover route between Santa Fe, New Mexico and Arizpe, Sonora

1787   released as governor at his own request; assumes command of Buenaventura Presidio

1788   given command of Tucson Presidio; dies suddenly on December 19

TIMELINE IN HISTORY

1602   Sebastián Vizcaíno discovers Monterey

1732   George Washington is born

1735   freedom of the press recognized with the acquittal of printer John Peter Zenger

1743   Thomas Jefferson is born

1756   Seven Years War, also known as The French and Indian War, begins

1763   after its loss in the French and Indian War, France gives Canada and all territory east of the Mississippi to England

1767   Mason-Dixon Line is established between Maryland and Pennsylvania; Jesuits are expelled from California

1769   Daniel Boone explores route through the Cumberland Gap; Father Junípero Serra founds Mission San Diego de Alcalá, the first Franciscan California mission; Portolá expedition departs San Diego in search of Monterey

1770   Boston Massacre

1773   Boston Tea Party

1775   American Revolution begins with battles at Lexington and Concord

1776   signing of Declaration of Independence

1781   first non-native settlers arrive in Los Angeles

1783   Treaty of Paris ends the American Revolution

1787   Constitutional Convention ratifies U.S. Constitution

1789   George Washington inaugurated as first U.S. President

1812   Russians establish settlement in California at Bodega Bay, north of San Francisco

1841   Russians leave California

1848   California given to U.S. after end of Mexican-American War

1849   California Gold Rush begins

1850   California joins the Union as the 31st state

1912   Arizona joins the Union as the 48th state

FOR FURTHER READING

For Young Adults:

Doherty, Kieran. *Explorers, Missionaries and Trappers*. Minneapolis, MN: The Oliver Press, Inc., 2000.

Hatt, Christine. *The American West: Native Americans, Pioneers and Settlers*. New York: Peter Bedric Books, 1998.

Lauritzen, Jonreed. *Colonel Anza's Important Journey*. New York: G.P. Putnam Sons, 1966.

Smith, Carter (editor). *Exploring the Frontier*. Brookfield, CT: Millbrook Press, 1992.

Works Consulted:

Bolton, Herbert Eugene. *An Outpost of Empire*. New York: Russell and Russell, 1966.

_____. *Anza's California Expeditions*. (5 vols). Berkeley: University of California Press, 1930.

Bowman, J.N. and Robert F. Heizer. *Anza and the Northwest Frontier of Spain*. Los Angeles: Southwest Museum, 1967.

Hook, Jason. *The Apaches*. Oxford, England: Osprey Publishing, 1987.

Pourade, Richard F. *Anza Conquers the Desert*. San Diego, CA: Union Tribune Publishing, 1971.

Reedstrom, E. Lisle. *Apache Wars: An Illustrated Battle History*. New York: Sterling Publishing Company, Inc., 1990.

ON THE WEB

Juan Bautista de Anza, 1735-1788
http://www.linkline.com/personal/shoe62/anza/jba.html

Juan Bautista de Anza Blazed the Anza Trail
http://www.desertusa.com/magjan98/jan_pap/du_anza.html

Juan Bautista de Anza National Historic Trail
http://www.nps.gov/juba

The History of San Diego: The Explorers
http://sandiegohistory.org/books/pourade/explorers/explorers.htm

Tubac Through Four Centuries
http://dizzy.library.arizona.edu/images/dobyns/

Web de Anza
http://anza.uoregon.edu/

GLOSSARY

adobe (ah-DOH-bee) - brick made from mixture of water, clay and straw, then dried in the sun

conquistador (con-KEEST-ah-door) - early Spanish explorer; especially one who conquered vast portions of territory in the New World

hapless (HAP-less) - unfortunate, having bad luck

league (LEEG) - unit of measurement of about three miles

missions (MISH-uns) - church or settlement areas where priests worked to convert native tribes to the Christian religion

New World - North, South, and Central America (The "Old World" was whatever was known to Europeans in the 15th century)

presidio (preh-SID-ee-oh) - Spanish fort

scurvy (SKUR-vee) - disease caused by lack of vitamin C (found mainly in fruits like oranges and lemons) which causes bleeding beneath the skin and weakness. Especially common on long sea voyages, and many sailors died from it

strait (STRATE) - narrow passage connecting two bodies of water

treaty (TREE-tee) - contract between two nations or groups of people to ensure peaceful relations

tundra (TUN-druh) - treeless area that can only support vegetation such as moss

vaquero (vaw-CARE-oh) - Spanish word meaning cowboy or herdsman

viceroy (VICE-uh-roy) - Spanish governor

INDEX